FORMOSA

By Trey Dees

JEC PUBLISHING COMPANY

2969 E. Chestnut Expy
Springfield, Missouri 65802
(800) 313-5121
www.jecpubco.com

Copyright © 2010 by Trey Dees

Library of Congress Control Number: 2010920137

ISBN: 978-0-9824801-9-9

Author: Trey Dees

Cover Design by: John Sager
Proofed and Edited by: Pam Eddings
Prepared for Publishing by: JE Cornwell

All rights reserved.
This publication; *Formosa* its content and cover are the property of Trey Dees. This book or parts thereof, may not be reproduced in any form without permission from Trey Dees or JEC Publishing Co; exceptions are made for printed reviews and advertising and marketing excerpts.

Dedication:

To my beloved grandmother; Ladene Needham Halbrook Dees, without whose love and knowledge I would have never been able to complete this book. She has been gone from my life for ten years, but this story has been in my mind and soul for thirty years. I will love and remember her, Always.

Acknowledgments:

My Uncle Austin and Aunt Judy taught me a love for reading and writing. It was through their influence that I began compiling the information for this book.

I would like to thank Raymond Morgan for his help with this book. He has been a great step-father to me, and I greatly appreciate him.

I also want to thank Angie Morgan, my mom, for her help with this book.

I thank my beloved little daughter, Danyelle, for her never-ending inspiration of hope and support. She is ten years old and lives in Star City, AR with her grandparents, Raymond and Angie Morgan.

My other grandmother, Laverne Brown Barker lives in El Dorado, AR. She is my last remaining grandparent, and is a beautiful lady inside and out. She is a major love of my life.

I pay tribute to my grandfathers, Harry Dees and Earnest Sawyer, the greatest men of my life.

I also want to mention my girlfriend, Carmen White, who has put up with my singing and writing career. She has lived with my chaotic life, and all my ups and downs. I love her for staying with me.

My final acknowledgment goes to my dad, Harry Dees Jr., who was the first baby of my beloved grandmother. I was the second, and I appreciate him for stepping aside and letting me be her baby also. This book will be special to both of us because we were both completely in love with her.

God Bless the Halbrooks, Needhams, Sawyers, Browns, and Dees families.

I love you all!

Introduction

Stories about the Ozarks in the 1930s were reminiscent of a great time in history. My families were a significant part of this history. The Halbrooks and Needhams, trying to escape the evils of the Civil War, transplanted their families from McNairy County, Tennessee into Van Buren County, Arkansas in the early 1860s. The burning of the South was a very sad time, but the move provided my family a chance to start fresh in a safer state. The second generation of these families lived to experience the changes of facing a wild wilderness, the First World War, and the Great Depression.

The Ozarks area is a spooky and mysterious, yet magical place. At this time in history it was very remote, but full of loving Christian families who were tested by hard times. I am proud that my family was part of this time in history. These stories are only a few of many that were never told. The stories of my grandmother have been in my heart for many years, and now this book is allowing me to share those memories from her life. The adventures recounted in Formosa take place in the heart of our country and consist of ups and downs, incredible thrill rides that may cause you to wonder if such things could be true, but I assure you, they are.

Table of Contents

1. Grandma Needham 11
2. Lightfoot, The Terror From Wolverton Mountain 20
3. Drama at Choctaw School 31
4. Autumn in the Ozarks 39
5. Fishing and the Church House 48
6. Holiday Hills 53
7. Twister at Bee Branch 65
8. Spring Time, Finally 69
9. Blood on Wolverton Mountain 77
10. The World is Changing for Uncle Oscar 83
11. A Year in the Life of an Ozark Girl 87

Chapter One

Grandma Needham

"Hurry up," I said, "Grandma will be waiting for us." They were both trying to scramble out of the creek, but kept slipping on the rocks. I half-heartedly laughed as I turned to see a wagon coming around the bend across the bridge. It was Eddie Crabtree, an old hillbilly boy from over at Center Ridge. Just when he got about dead center of Old Piney, he stopped the horses and started gawking. I looked down at Erma Lea and Dana, and both of them were standing ankle deep in the creek. I hollered at them to get back in the water.

Grandma Needham

Dana said, "You just told us to get out!"

I knew there was no reasoning with those two; they're as naive as a newborn baby chicken. But Eddie, on the other hand, was about sixteen or seventeen, and he knew he was just being a big old pest. My temper swelled so that I grabbed three or four perfectly round creek rocks and took a pitcher's stance. "Eddie," I yelled, "Boy you got just three seconds to get that team moving or you're gonna get it."

He looked at me like I was nothing but a young girl, but he doesn't know me very well. The first rock hit the wagon wheel with a loud thud. Eddie broke out of his trance and hollered for his team to get up. The next rock flew past his big ear, and the third rock hit the younger horse right on his rear end. Being young and restless, he was just aching for a reason to run, and buddy that was it. Eddie fell backward and landed in the back of the wagon. Those two horses took off like an automobile. As they rounded the corner, Eddie was hollering and trying to get back in the driver's seat. I could hear them, running wide open, headed for Choctaw Feed Store.

There was a moment of silence, then I doubled over with laughter. I looked over at them, but they

Chapter 1

weren't laughing.

"Why did you do that?" Dana asked.

"Well, he was looking at both of you," I said.

"What," Dana said.

"Well you know what I mean; he was looking at you in a bad way," I said.

The two looked at each other and then at me with a puzzled look.

I said disgustedly, "Let's go." I am only two years older than Dana and one year older than Erma Lea, but I've always seemed to be more schooled about the world. Sometimes I think about how nice it would be to be so naive about life the way that they are. They just float through life carefree. But me, I'm only twelve, but I already act grown. I seem to know life very well and what can and will happen. Mama always says that it's my Indian blood; the Cherokee people run strong in me. Perhaps that's so because you always have to have a good balance in the world. The serious and comedians, the leaders and followers, the wise and ridiculous - all make the world go 'round.

When we arrived back at Formosa, grandma was sweeping off her porch. We started up the driveway, and she waved a hand to hurry up. "Let's go pick some blackberries," she yelled. She didn't

Grandma Needham

have to tell us twice. We all looked at each other and took off in a dead run. Grandma put on her bonnet, and we grabbed our little buckets and fell in behind her. We all headed over toward the Halbrook Cemetery. It's our family cemetery and sits upon a little hill with huge oak trees scattered throughout it. Beautiful fields surround the cemetery for a mile in each direction.

When we got over by the cemetery, Grandma told us to watch for copperheads. "You know those little orange and yellow devils will get you," she told us.

We got our buckets plum' full of the sweetest blackberries in the country. "Grandma, I said, "Will you make cobbler with them?"

"Sure will honey," she said.

"And Grandma, what if Whitey gets after us while we're on our way back home?" I asked.

"You let me worry about that," she said. When we got about halfway across the field, here he came. "Take off," she yelled at us.

We ran as fast as we could go, trying not to spill our blackberries or get in a sticker bed. Of course we were barefooted. All the kids in these hills go barefooted in the summer time. Right before school starts, we all get a brand new pair of shoes.

Chapter 1

That Brahma bull ran right up to Grandma. By gosh, it looked like David and Goliath. That old humped-back bull weighed at least a thousand pounds and stood six or seven feet tall. Grandma was short and stubby, standing four feet eleven and about a hundred sixty pounds. When Goliath attacked David, he got killed because David's little rock hit his only weak spot, right between his eyes. Well, Grandma got the bull's only weak spot, right on his pink and black nose. He ran right up to her like he was gonna hook or head-butt her, but when he looked up, she popped his nose with a thick little hickory switch. That bull turned and ran off, bellowing in pain. We all started cheering for Grandma as she hurried across the field. Now see, this old bull had been chasing us girls for two years. So it was time that Grandma got even.

We set our buckets on the porch and started picking stickers out of our feet when we heard the God awfulest noise in the world. Around the house came Ole Red, and he was dragging the plow and Uncle Oscar all at the same time. He was running as fast as a mule could run under those circumstances. About the time they hit the peach orchard, Uncle Oscar rolled free. He came up out of the dust cursing like a sailor! Ole Red

Grandma Needham

went on another hundred feet and got hung up in a briar thicket. Uncle Oscar walked toward him like he was in a gunfight. Old Red just stood still as a statue, waiting. Uncle Oscar walked up to Ole Red and punched him in the jaw so hard it sounded like someone hit a piece of wood with an axe. It staggered Ole Red, but when he shook it off, both of them walked back to the cornfield. Ole Red and Uncle Oscar have a thing between them where they see which one is more ornery, and to tell you the truth, I don't know which one it is.

Uncle Oscar is quite a character. He's my Mama's older brother. He's six-two and two hundred pounds of strong bone and muscle. He's a more solid man than you will find anywhere in these hills. He's got strong Cherokee blood running through his veins. Even Old Red knows when to stop pushing him around. Uncle Oscar is the strong and silent type, very serious and very honest - all about business. Just like when he and Ole Red walked past the porch, he didn't even acknowledge us sitting there. But he knew we were, because he hollered back and told us he had a big ole watermelon for us, cooling down in the spring water.

Mama's side of the family are country folks;

Chapter 1

Needham is their name. A great grandfather of ours, James Alfred Needham, was the first white man to move into Tennessee. Back in the late 1600's, he had entered Tennessee with the intention of living among the Cherokee and making land deals. So our family spent a hundred-fifty years in Tennessee before moving to Arkansas in the eighteen-fifties. Grandma was the first Needham born here in the Ozarks.

The new families that settled here named the county after one of the former presidents, Van Buren. The hills were very wild in those days - there were bears and wolves everywhere. Grandma said that you couldn't go out at night because the wolves would get you. "A hunter would kill a bear every day of the week, as easily as killing a squirrel," she'd say. She always liked telling one particular tale about a rogue black bear that was so big he tore the door off the hinges but couldn't fit through the doorway. Her dad was away on a hunting and trapping adventure when this happened. Since there were no men around and her mother was in the bed with an illness, Grandma loaded up an old muzzle loader and shot that bear in the belly. That bear was so mad, his eyes were red like fire. He wanted to tear her apart but couldn't fit through that door.

Grandma Needham

She started loading that muzzle loader up again, but the bear's belly started burning from the first shot, so he took off like a jackrabbit, hollering and bellowing and tearing up everything in his path. She said grinning, "That old bear must have weighed over five hundred pounds, and the funny thing is, he never came back." About dusk we finished supper and started on the watermelon that Uncle Oscar had for us.

"Oscar will be taking you girls home," Grandma said.

"Aw, we can walk, Grandma," Erma Lea said.

"No," Grandma said sternly. "Not today."

I was curious as we got up on the wagon. Grandma was acting kind of annoyed about something. I looked down and saw Uncle Oscar's Forty-Four Winchester between his knees. About a mile down the road, I asked him what was wrong.

He looked at me out of the corner of his eye and said, "Lightfoot is back." That word was enough to make my heart stop. "I want you girls to be careful until he's gone; no walking back and forth between your house and mine. I'll tell your dad what's going on."

For the next couple of miles back home, I was spooked. Every shadow seemed to be alive, and

Chapter 1

every noise made me jump. There was a lump in my throat, and my hair stood on end until we came into Choctaw. We passed the store and the school and headed up to our place. Dad was in the front yard, washing his new Chevrolet. He was so proud of it. Dad was one of only a handful of people that had a car. Most of the people had horses and buggies. The depression was only three years old, and most folks didn't even know what money looked like. Dad owned the only store in Choctaw, so that gave us a little more money than most other folks around these parts.

Chapter Two

Lightfoot, The Terror From Wolverton Mountain

Dad told us all to come on in and get some supper. Uncle Oscar hung up his hat and sat down and filled his plate so full it looked like it was going to run over. Just as he sunk his fork in and aimed toward his mouth, Mama yelled, "No you don't, we'll have the blessing first." Dad stood up and led us in a beautiful prayer, the same way he leads us every Sunday down at Choctaw Church of Christ.

Dad's people are the Halbrooks, city folks

Chapter 2

from up in Clinton, our county seat. They are all educated, but down-to-earth, good Christian people.

After supper, we all relaxed around the living room. Dad and Uncle Oscar were in rocking chairs smoking their pipes when Uncle Oscar told Dad that Lightfoot was back.

"Are you sure?" Dad asked.

"Of course," Uncle Oscar said. "He got one of my little pigs two days ago." It got dead quiet for a few minutes. All that could be heard was the squeaking of the rocking chairs. Then Uncle Oscar went into one of Lightfoot's tales.

~~~~~

"I was hunting at the base of Wolverton Mountain when I first saw him. I couldn't make out what it was at first. It was black like a bear, but I knew it wasn't a bear. It was too small for that; it was short and long and had a tail as long as it was. It made no sound at all and moved so slowly and smoothly, it looked like a shadow at dusk. As I watched it twitch its tail around nervously, my blood ran cold because I was sure what it was. I had never actually seen one, but had heard the old-timers tell tales about how they could outfight a pack of wolves, were more aggressive than a black bear, and so smart that they could slip in and kill right under your nose, and you would never know they were there.

"The legend of the panther is very big; it stretches from coast to coast, but they were thought to be extinct here in this state because they were hunted purely out of hatred. They range in color from brown to gray to black; they weigh from a hundred pounds to twice that, and are lightning fast and as smart as any man.

"Nobody had seen a panther in this area for over twenty years when I saw Lightfoot. It seemed like an hour that he just stood there looking toward my direction. I was so amazed that I didn't realize he was headed straight for my farm, and when you've got a big cat headed towards your farm, it spells out trouble.

"It was a gamble, but I had only a second to decide, so I hammered my forty-four and aimed for his lungs. Unfortunately, the trouble with a cat is that they are so double-jointed you can hardly tell where their shoulder is. I squeezed the trigger and before I could blink, he did a somersault and was gone back up Wolverton Mountain - like a lightning flash he was gone.

"I had hoped to get a good clean lung shot, but hope faded when I couldn't find any good pink lung

Chapter 2

blood. I must have hit him in the muscle and gristle of his shoulder. Now the cat was really dangerous, because a wounded panther can't catch wild animals, so they strictly depend on livestock.

"So this was the beginning of Lightfoot wreaking havoc upon the people of Van Buren County. He would move around and raid farms because he was too smart for traps; he would dig around and up under them and flip them over. He could figure out poisonous meat; he'd lie and wait for an old 'possum to start eating on the bait to see if it was poisoned. If the men got too tired of it, they'd get together with their best hunting dogs and take out after him. It would usually last a week or so - a lot of drinking mostly, but every once in awhile they'd catch up to him. It always ended up with a few dead dogs and a bunch of ole tired hillbillies."

Uncle Oscar lit his pipe again and continued, "About two years ago the elders got together and hired some professional hunters from Louisiana. I told them it was a bad idea; hog hunting was dangerous for sure, but nothing was like hunting a big cat because they can deal death from five different sources. Hogs have deadly tusks, but they don't have four paws full of razor sharp one-inch claws. But they didn't listen to me - naturally they hired these men for five hundred dollars; they would receive half when they arrived and the other half when they brought the dead Lightfoot into town. That's more than a year's wages just to kill a cat, but Lightfoot was not just an ordinary cat; he was part demon.

"When the Cajuns arrived, they were surely a sight - long beards and big rimmed hats - their broken English was so hard you couldn't understand them. They had four plott hounds and two big muscled-up pit bull dogs. Man, those dogs were nothing but muscle and scars, clipped tails and ears. Those dogs were as tough and mean looking as the men were. Everyone figured if anyone could kill Lightfoot, it would be this bunch. They were a true fighting crew. That Louisiana swamp country must be very rough because the men and dogs reflected it. Everyone around here was betting on the action; that is, everyone but me. I just couldn't bet on bloodshed; I told them that I didn't know for sure of the outcome. But I was willing to bet that when it was all said and done, Lightfoot would be the one still standing. Of course, the Cajuns bragged about what their dogs would do to Lightfoot, but I just wasn't so sure about that.

"For the first two weeks, Lightfoot just toyed

Chapter 2

with them - the hounds cold-trailed, and when they did pick up the trail, it led them in a big circle. It would lead them right back to where they had started just hours before. It was all a bad mess because the Cajuns were from flat lands - these Ozarks are only three thousand feet at the max, but it's usually straight up and down, and Lightfoot knew every inch of it. The men and dogs were worn out. You could see them camped along different farms - their old truck, a tent and a campfire. They slept during the day and hunted every night. The residents of the county would inform them which farms that Lightfoot was attacking. They would get the dogs out at a fresh kill and start the hunt - I guess Lightfoot got tired of them spoiling his plans because on the third week he got violent with them. The fall moon was full, yellow and spooky, a panther's moon! Lightfoot allowed the lead hound to get within seeing distance. When the hound was within a hundred feet, Lightfoot made a big circle and came out upon a huge rock which brought him twenty feet above the trail. When the lead hound came under the big rock, Lightfoot came down with two hundred pounds of fury and snapped the dog's back. The dog moaned in fear and agony for a few minutes as Lightfoot circled him. The Cajuns were

Lightfoot, The Terror From Wolverton Mountain

five hundred feet down the trail and could hear and see everything that was going on - the bulldogs were going crazy, wanting to come to the aid of their comrade, but the Cajuns would not release them that far away. If they had, the dogs would be worn out by the time they reached the fight scene. They were made for fighting, not running, so they remained on their leashes. When the men and dogs were directly below and in perfect view, Lightfoot acted in a flash. He grabbed the hound and slung him off the cliff. The men watched in horror as their best dog came tumbling end over end down the mountain, coming to a stop right in front of the men - every bone in his body was broken. The cat looked down and screamed, a piercing, defiant sound that echoed down the valley, and then he turned and vanished. It was a warning to leave him alone, but the hunters didn't heed it. As word spread around town, the bets just increased. The tension rose as the Cajuns swore they would skin the cat alive, to make him suffer as much as possible.

"Six days later they got another chance; this time the night was as black as coal. You could hardly see your hand in front of your face, not a breeze could be felt. The dogs bayed about midnight - the men rushed up Wolverton Mountain, and this

Chapter 2

time it was personal. They were fueled up about the death of their best dog - even the bulldogs were fired up. The men were so sure about themselves that they could already picture themselves parading Lightfoot around Choctaw and collecting the rest of their money. When they reached the cave's entrance, the three hounds were so excited that their barking sounded like one continuous bay. The bulldogs were released, and they shot into the cave like bullets. For about five minutes they wandered around and around - the men knew he had to be in there because their hounds never lie. The men started hollering at the bulldogs, telling them to attack. One bulldog started jumping up into the air, his jaws slapping together like a steel trap. After the third jump, his body seemed to freeze in midair and started shaking vigorously. The other bulldog looked on in bewilderment as did the Cajuns. In less than a minute, his white body fell to the cave floor like a sack of bricks. In a flash the other bulldog was lifted off the cave floor and also began shaking vigorously. The Cajuns were so spooked, they thought this might be black magic - they were very familiar with such, being from Louisiana. Within a minute, the second dog fell to the floor and lay there shaking. The three hounds took off

Lightfoot, The Terror From Wolverton Mountain

like rabbits - they ran into one of the Cajuns so hard that he stumbled backward and almost fell off the cliff that went straight down. He dropped his rifle off the cliff, and his lantern hit the limestone with such force that it burst into a huge flame that lit up the mountainside. They dropped to one knee, trapped between the cave and the cliff's edge - they peered into the cave and saw the bodies of their two dead bulldogs. The one Cajun who still had his rifle started shooting at shadows, everywhere he saw a flicker of movement, he levered in a shell and shot at it. Just as the flame's light almost faded, they both looked up thirty feet above their heads and saw two yellow eyes looking down at them - they didn't blink, they just glared like demon's eyes, and they didn't seem real. Then came a piercing scream that ripped the night apart - as it was still echoing, a second followed as if a warning to leave him alone, a warning of defiance. All they could see were yellow eyes and white fangs. Then as the Cajun raised his rifle to fire, the cat disappeared. The flame died down, and all the excitement was suddenly over - as quickly as it started, it all stopped. The night was black and quiet once again - the men ran down Wolverton Mountain as fast as they could. They knocked on my door about two in the

Chapter 2

morning, and I swear they were as pale as ghosts. They told me what had happened, ate breakfast, got their belongings and got out of town. Their three hounds lay in the back of their truck, shivering like babies. It was the damnedest thing I had ever seen. I told them I would go up there and bury their dogs; they simply said, 'Thank you' and left the county.

"I went up on Wolverton around noon - I could see how Lightfoot so easily killed the dogs; his cave was a series of chambers with one big entrance that led up to a smaller cave and then to an even smaller one, and then to an entrance in the top that was just big enough for a cat or a man. He could enter or escape at either end. Inside the lower level was a ledge about five feet off the floor - it went all around the cave, and Lightfoot could kill the bulldogs at his leisure, without risking his own life. He just sunk his claws into their shoulders and lifted them off the cave floor and worked on them. He broke their necks and then dropped them when he realized there was no life left in them. This was apparent by the deep claw marks in their shoulders and the teeth marks in their necks. Sixty pounds was nothing for a two-hundred pound panther to pick up off the ground. Lightfoot killed these dogs so easily he didn't get a scratch, and he was so smart he slipped away and probably wouldn't return until the pressure was off. That cat has the strongest sixth sense of any animal I've ever seen. I buried the dogs, and with one last look around so as to get a mental picture of the place - I turned and got off Wolverton Mountain."

Chapter 3

Chapter Three

Drama At Choctaw School

When Dad touched me, I almost jumped through my skin. I was on the couch and had drifted off to sleep about the time Uncle Oscar was finishing the story. Dad told me to get up and go to bed. I scooped little Sammy off the couch as Uncle Oscar was grabbing his rifle and hat and leaving through the door.

That night I drifted off to dream about blackberries, green fields, bulls and panthers. Suddenly, I awoke and sat straight up in the bed. What had awakened me? I looked out of my

Drama at Choctaw School

window, and across the valley I could see a little color in the sky that allowed me to see the outline of Sugarloaf Mountain to the east. I could barely see little Red River down in the valley, but I could hear it flowing very loudly. It's a beautiful sound to hear a mountain stream flowing.

I looked down at the ground and wondered if a panther could jump this high and climb through a window. I have to admit that Uncle Oscar's stories of Lightfoot surely spooked me, but I knew that Lightfoot never came this far over. I also knew that he never came near town, and we lived at the edge of town. He always attacked out in the country; besides, he was the only panther around these parts as far as anyone knew. As mean as he was, it was sad to think of him being the only one. To be all alone is a terrible thing; I can't imagine what it would be like to be the only human, and have to live with the knowledge that all of your kind was finished in this area. I don't know why he didn't go and find his own kind. But Uncle Oscar said he was born on Wolverton Mountain and would probably die there. That's probably right because Wolverton Mountain has always been a place of legend, a place of spooks and ghost stories.

I felt around for little Sammy, and got hold of

Chapter 3

his arm. I had forgotten he was there until I heard him breathing. I remembered when Mama got pregnant with him; there is nine years between him and Dana. Mama thought she couldn't get pregnant anymore; I remember she cried a lot. But what you think of as a mistake could be a blessing in disguise, for now he is Mama's little baby, spoiled as can be. Mama has asked the Lord to forgive her a hundred times over for not wanting another child. Dad always told her that the Lord knows best, that we can't see the whole picture like He can.

It was daylight when Dad awoke us; Mama had a great breakfast as usual - biscuits, gravy, ham, bacon and eggs. Dad was worried about us going to Grandma's while Lightfoot was on the warpath, so I worked in the store for the next month until school started. Dad wanted me to learn the business that he was so proud of. "It's a great thing to serve the people," he always said, and he had it down to an art. Dad had such love and compassion for people; he was the only man I knew who could go to the funeral of someone he didn't know and cry like a baby. That's my dad, he's a wonderful man.

The first day of school was sunny and warm. Dana and I got our lunch pails and headed for school. We live right next door to the schoolhouse.

Drama at Choctaw School

It's just down a little hill, through a little patch of woods, up another hill, and there it sits - just two hundred yards from our house. When we got to school, Erma Lea was waiting on us. Dana broke away from us and headed for her classroom. She's two grades below us. Erma Lea is nearly a year younger than me, but we're in the same grade. She is very tall for her age and very smart. Her dad and my Mama are first cousins. So that makes us second or third cousins or something like that.

The day seemed like it would never end, but it's always like that on the first day of school. When it finally ended, we waited out front for Dana for nearly twenty minutes. I looked at my watch again and told Erma Lea to go around the right side of the school, and I would go around the left side. Just as we started, here came Dana, walking fast and looking back. Acting scared, she said, "Let's go."

"What's wrong?" I asked.

"Nothing, let's go," she said.

When we got home and started throwing the softball around, she relaxed and told me that a mean bully was picking on her. I felt the blood run to my face. She could see my look change.

"That's why I didn't tell you," she said. "I knew you would go crazy just like Mama."

Chapter 3

She was right. I could feel my famous Needham temper start to rise. The thought of someone being mean to sweet, pretty little Dana made me get crazy mad. Everybody knows that Mama is like that. She's very calm and quiet, but you had better not do anything dirty to her!

Once Mama got it in her mind that she was going to vote. Everyone except Mama knew a woman couldn't vote. Anything a man could do, she could do better. So she made Dad carry her up to Clinton during the election. Mama just walked in and proceeded to vote.

The mayor approached her awkwardly and said, "Clara, women can't vote, you know that." But, that was the wrong thing to say to her.

She took off on a dead run to Dad's car and grabbed her softball bat. Mama is only about one hundred-twenty pounds, but she made up for it with that bat. She proceeded to bust the ballot boxes up, and every time a man would try to grab her, she would take a swing at his head. After ten minutes or so, the anger wore off, and reality set in. She looked around at the disaster area and about two dozen angry male faces. Dad was sitting in the corner after he had tried to grab Mama - she had taken a swing at him too. It was as silent as a library, and the

Drama at Choctaw School

tension was building. Mama realized the trouble she had caused. She grabbed Dad by the arm and pulled him out the door of the courthouse. Just as she got through the doorway, she turned and yelled, "If any of you try to do anything to me, Oscar will come after you!" She knew that would stop any intentions of theirs. Mama was so embarrassed after it all, that she didn't go back to Clinton for over two years - that's Mama for you.

Right this moment, I was feeling just like Mama. I couldn't control my anger. I was wondering what this girl looked like, how big she was and why she had enough nerve to pick on Dana. "Who does she think she is? Tomorrow she'll find out how wrong she is, to pick on my family!"

The next morning I practically ran to school. Dana was yelling at me to slow down. I couldn't; I was boiling inside. All day I was a brewing pot. Everything got on my nerves, and I couldn't concentrate. Nobody could talk to me. Erma Lea asked what was wrong and I said, "You know!" She just shook her head yes.

When the bell rang at three, I was the first one out in the hall and halfway down, I ran into a mob. Erma Lea was right on my heels. We worked our way through five hundred students, from the first

Chapter 3

through the twelfth grades. After nearly fifteen minutes of working through, I emerged into the open, just twenty feet away from the outhouses. There were two girls holding Dana's arms, and a heavy-set girl with long, curly blond hair was squeezing Dana's cheeks together real hard. Her left hand had Dana by the dress. I could see big tears swelling in Dana's eyes. I dropped my bag and books and squatted into a running position. I felt like that mean old white Brahma bull that chases us over at Grandma's. Just as I was fixin' to take off, Erma Lea burst through the crowd and ran right square into my back. She hit me so hard, it threw me forward. I just went with it and used the momentum to my benefit. I hit that girl like a football tackle. I had one arm around her waist and a handful of hair with the other. My shoulder slammed into her rib cage, and it took the air out of her. I twisted hard to the right and slung her as hard as I could. The impact was so great it sent Dana and the other two girls rolling in the dirt. As for the big girl, she rolled down the hill right into the sewer pit. She went under and came back up screaming. But nobody was jumping forward to get her out. I stumbled, but managed to get my footing. That girl was waist-deep in that nasty crap. I took one quick

Drama at Choctaw School

look around, grabbed Dana and Erma Lea, and we took off before the teachers got there. Hundreds of kids were staring at her in a hush. I had never heard so many kids be that quiet before. I looked back and saw two teachers helping her out of the mess. We quickly rushed into the house and changed our clothes to play softball. Every kid knows that the best thing to do is to hurry and act innocent! Never admit to anything unless absolutely necessary!

I was changing when Mama walked into my room. She put her hands on her hips and calmly said, "Dana told me what happened. You did the same thing I would have done. I'm proud of you. We won't let your Dad know about this, okay? Because you know he doesn't approve of violence under any circumstances."

You know, Mama and I have never been close. She's close to Dana and Sammy. I'm a daddy's girl, but at that moment, I felt Mama and I became lifelong friends.

Chapter Four

Autumn In The Ozarks

The big October Moons are beautiful in Arkansas. They seem sort of magical. The whole landscape is bathed in moonlight, and you can see like in daylight. This is one of my favorite times of the year. All animals become nocturnal at this time of the year, and this is the time of the year that Lightfoot becomes the most dangerous. During the fall, he wreaks havoc upon every farm in the county. He works everyone into such a frenzy! Dad told us during supper that Lightfoot had killed a pig over at Uncle Oscar's farm. Uncle Oscar found the pig underneath a big ole bull pine tree, buried in a shallow grave. That's how a panther does it - it buries its kill and usually comes back to feed over two or three days.

By the light of the big full moon Uncle Oscar climbed up a white oak tree, wrapped a wool blanket around himself, laid his rifle across his lap and waited for Lightfoot. Around midnight he spotted a shadow that wasn't there before. He looked away and then looked back - the shadow had moved. It was Lightfoot! He hammered the forty-four. Lightfoot heard it and looked around. Panthers can see as good at night as in daylight. And their senses are much more powerful than human's. As Uncle Oscar was getting a bead on him, he noticed that huge tail starting to nervously twitch around. That was something that Lightfoot seemed to do when he became nervous or angry. At the instant that he fired, Lightfoot jumped. He knew that he had missed. But he continued to shoot into the dark anyway. He put half a dozen slugs into the direction that Lightfoot went. He knew he wouldn't hit him, but would let the cat know he was wise to him! He climbed down out of the huge white oak and headed for the house. He didn't check for blood since he was sure he hadn't hit the cat. A man doesn't kill a

Chapter 4

panther with luck; it takes time and skill. It would take more than normal measures to kill this one since he wasn't by any means a normal panther.

The next weekend we all went to stay with Grandma. Ole Man Webb was driving over from Birdtown with his redbone hounds that he was so proud of. We could hear them barking a mile away. He turned into Grandma's house. Those hounds' big ears were flopping in the wind, and their heads were hanging over the sides of the truck. All day long, Uncle Oscar and Ole Man Webb prepared for the big coon hunt. Those hounds barked all day long.

Grandma got so mad, she said, "Go feed those dang hounds before I shoot 'em." Both men oiled their guns, fueled up the lanterns and rested by the fireplace.

We finished supper, and sat by the fire as it popped and crackled.

Ole Man Webb said, "Sally, spin us a yarn."

Boy, Grandma was always ready for that. She wasted no time in starting. "It was sixty-three or four, and I was five or six then. I was a chunky little girl, a lot like I am now," she giggled. "The Yankees came through these hills after winning the battle over at Pea Ridge; then they went down and took Little Rock. We didn't want any part of this fighting.

Autumn in the Ozarks

It was all about black folks and cotton, and I had never seen either one. Those yanks poked me in the belly with their bayonets. It didn't break the skin, but it sure did hurt. They thought I was wearing a money pouch.

"They raided our farms, took our money, jewelry and food. I know it happened on both sides - it's the spoils of war. During war, it's the common people who suffer.

I didn't know a single man from this county that fought during the Great War. But we got some little critters around here that did some fighting. A group of blue coats headed down to Little Rock to relieve a tired regiment that had been there since the taking of our capital. Just as they got below Bee Branch, they decided to camp for the night. Sometime that evening, a mule or horse or something stirred up a yellow jacket's nest! Boy, those little yellow devils went to work on those blue bellies! Men and horses were headed in all directions! It was Conway before they rounded everything up! We whopped 'em and didn't fire a shot!" Grandma rolled with laughter.

It was about ten o'clock, so the men got their lanterns lit, put the four hounds on leashes and headed for the woods - you know, every man in these hills coon hunts. And every little boy grows

Chapter 4

up wanting to get some good coon dogs and be a good hunter himself. A lot of city folks think that coon hunting is a cruel sport - all those big ole dogs on one little coon. Most coon dogs weigh at least seventy pounds, and a full grown coon is only thirty or forty pounds; sometimes there might be eight or ten dogs on one little coon. But, brother, that little coon will sometimes whop the whole pack of dogs and go on home. A lot of hunters will let 'em go if they can do it. Despite the belief of city folks, hunters are mostly a group of honest, fun-loving people, and they are the most sportsmanlike people on earth. City people see the little raccoon in zoos and pictures and think he's sweet and cute. But they don't know the hill coon. Pound for pound, he's the greatest fighter on earth. All you have to do is look at coon hounds. Their heads and necks are all scarred up from a lifetime of coon hunting. Ole Man Webb's dogs looked a sight once you got close to them. If a hound ever makes the mistake of getting into water with a coon, he'll get drowned nine times out of ten. Coons have an art of getting on a dog and holding his head under the water. Coons are excellent swimmers, and they wash everything they eat - they're extra clean, wonderful animals.

By one o'clock, the dogs had gotten three coons.

Autumn in the Ozarks

It was looking real good up 'til this point. The hounds had suddenly gotten quiet.

Uncle Oscar asked, "What direction are the dogs in?"

Ole Man Webb said, "I don't know, seems like northwest, maybe Wolverton Mountain."

"That's what I thought," Uncle Oscar said and cursed under his breath.

Ole Man Webb asked, "Is that bad?"

Uncle Oscar said, "It is for your dogs; you better hope Lightfoot hasn't killed all of 'em. You had better pray he ain't home tonight. Let's go!"

The two men hurried up the mountain side. It's two thousand feet up to the top of Wolverton Mountain; then it levels out flat, just like bottom land. You forget that you're on a mountaintop until you look out at the fields and valleys below. But, that's typical of the Ozark Mountains.

Uncle Oscar and Old Man Webb entered into a burnt-over clearing. Lightning must have started a fire up there, but before it spread over a quarter of a mile, rain had put it out. All the bigger trees were gone, and there was lots of underbrush and boulders. Limestone jutted out of the mountaintop in every direction. It was a terrible looking place - the men expected Lightfoot to be behind every rock

Chapter 4

or log. They stopped in the middle of the clearing and listened. They could make out the silhouettes of the dogs trailing around.

"Maggie girl," Ole Man Webb said. "Come here." He hooked Maggie to her leash. He was okay now. "Maggie's my baby," he said, "The brains of the outfit. As long as she's alright, I'm alright."

"Sit here with her Webb and wait on me," Uncle Oscar said. He unloaded all of his extra equipment, and with nothing but his Bowie knife and gun, he started forward with ghostlike movement. The hammer was back on his single shot twelve gauge, and he had his Bowie knife. Mountain men depend on their knives just as much as their rifles and shotguns. A hundred yards away, he found one of the hounds lying dead, its neck savagely broken - Lightfoot's work, for sure.

An eerie silence settled on the area. A little breeze had blown all night, but now none was blowing. It only added to the scariness of the situation. Another hundred yards further and something made the hair on Uncle Oscar's neck stand on end. There were three shadows in the night. One dog was with Ole Man Webb, and one was dead, leaving two dogs. But there were three silhouettes; the one to the far right suddenly leapt

Autumn in the Ozarks

upon the other two silhouettes. They tumbled twice, and then Lightfoot ran toward the edge of the mountain and vanished over the edge. Uncle Oscar saw why this animal was so dangerous; he killed the two hounds, covered fifty yards and vanished all in a span of fifteen seconds.

It all happened so fast he didn't have time to react. He quickly and cautiously crept to the edge of the mountain. Looking over the edge, two hundred feet below was the tree line. He knew Lightfoot hadn't made a mistake like going over the edge. But on closer observation, he spotted the narrow ledge below. This was Lightfoot's lair, the same place he had killed the bulldogs just two years before. Now, he knew what had happened - Lightfoot looked like he had gone over the edge of the mountain, but he had entered the small entrance into his cave. He remembered the entrance, but hadn't recognized it because it was burnt over. New underbrush had grown up and concealed the entrance that was already protected by the rocks.

When Uncle Oscar got back to Ole Man Webb, he realized the old man hadn't seen any of the drama that had taken place. He had been sitting on a log with his back to the action.

"Lightfoot killed your three male hounds, and

Chapter 4

he's in his cave," Uncle Oscar said.

"Did you go in after him?" Ole Man Webb asked.

"No, no man in his right mind would go into a panther's den and live to tell about it. I haven't ever been that stupid," Uncle Oscar said. "Let's get the hell off of this damn mountain!"

Chapter Five

Fishing And The Church House

After breakfast, we helped Mama wash the dishes; then we all got ready for church. Dad stopped by the Malone's house and picked up Erma Lea; then we headed over to Grandma's to get Uncle Oscar and Grandma. Dad had to poke some fun at Grandma, "Boy, it sure is a tight fit in here, isn't it, Sally?"

"It sure is Jim. I hate this noisy old contraption," she said.

"Well, we can always go back and get your wagon, although we'll get our clothes dirty, and

Chapter 5

church will be over by the time that we get there," Dad chuckled.

"I've had enough from you boy," she said.

Dad just laughed - he loved it.

We arrived right before ten o'clock. We all headed to the right side, all the way to the front. Dad went up and sat beside the pastor, back behind the pulpit. After the pastor welcomed everyone, Dad led us in song. Dad is the best male singer in the church, with a beautiful tenor voice. After the music, the pastor set into telling the story of Jonah and the whale. God had given Jonah a job to do. Instead of doing that job, Jonah got on a ship to another country. A huge storm came up, and the crew knew that God was mad at someone. When they found out it was Jonah, they threw him overboard. A huge whale came along and swallowed Jonah. He stayed in the whale's belly for three days and nights. But when he repented and agreed to do God's will, the great whale spat Jonah out onto dry ground. Everything acts in obedience to God's will, whether it's done the easy or hard way. It was a beautiful, but intense sermon. Everyone was on pins and needles. Without warning, the pastor slammed his fist down upon the pulpit, and all the old men and children jumped nearly straight up!

Fishing and the Church House

After church service, we stayed for Fifth Sunday eating. Oh man, what a delight! Every woman in the church competes with each other over fixin' food. They get awful jealous of each other, but all the men and kids sure take advantage of it.

After arriving home from the church dinner, Dad announced we'd go fishing. It was fall, but fairly warm and sunny. Besides, some of the best fishing was in the fall of the year. Dad's favorite pastime was fishing. Every chance he got, he'd go fishing. Next to us and the store, fishing was it. And Grandma wasn't far behind him; if she wasn't taking care of the farm, she wanted Dad to take her fishing.

During summertime, all the families in the area would camp out on Flat Rock. It was a huge rock base a hundred yards wide and just as long. It stretched right along the Little Red. It was a wonderful camping area; it was as flat as a board, and fifty wagons could fit on it. All the families had a great time on Flat Rock. Everyone would build fires, cook fish and potatoes, and run trotlines.

Grandma had set into her favorite fishing hole and had started catching little bream, just the size she enjoyed for a meal. Dad got to poking fun at her just at the instant she got a hold of a whopper.

Chapter 5

It played and pulled for ten minutes. When it got to the top, Dad saw it was an eel. Knowing Grandma hated snakes, Dad screamed out, "Sally, you got a good one, hold his head up; why it's the biggest snake I've ever seen!"

Grandma screamed and threw her pole into the river. She turned and grabbed another cane pole that was probably about twenty feet long. She caught Dad right across the backside as he was running up the hill! The commotion was so sudden and loud that all us kids came running over just in time to see Grandma pop Dad. He let out a yell and ran up the hill and laughed at the top of his lungs for five minutes. We all ran up to him and started laughing too.

"Go help Grandma and your mother get everything ready. I'm waiting at the car," he said.

On the way back to Grandma's, Dad showed us the welt on his lower back. "Dang you woman, you like to have killed me," he said. "Look at this welt," he laughed.

"Serves you right boy," Grandma grinned. They had the greatest relationship because they could pick on each other like that and it never got serious; besides, Dad was never serious anyway. The only thing Grandma and Mama feared in the world was a

Fishing and the Church House

snake. It just seemed to make their skins crawl.

It was after dark when we dropped Grandma off at the farm. All the way back to Choctaw, Dad told us stories about fishing when he was a little boy.

The big fall moon was coming up behind Sugarloaf Mountain. Dad stopped the car in the driveway and told us to sit still and just watch the moon rise. It was so beautiful because the orange of the sunset was still visible in the west while the moon was on the rise in the east. It always seems so magical this time of year.

Chapter 6

Chapter Six

Holiday Hills

When Thanksgiving rolled around, we were all in great spirits. Every year there was a big dance at Clinton that drew about a thousand people. When we pulled up, the music was cutting a rhythm out of the night. Most all my friends from school and their families were there. Dude Black's band was playing. They were the best bluegrass band in Arkansas. Dude traveled around the country playing for Bill Monroe when his band couldn't get work. We kids were all hanging around out back of the dance hall. The air was so crisp that I knew

Holiday Hills

it was going to snow. Mama and Dad had met at a dance like this twenty years ago. This was how most everyone in these hills met, at dances or at church socials. After the dance was over, we all covered up with blankets and sang all the way home.

The next day at school, Erma Lea came running up to me and yelling, "Dena, Dena."

"Calm down," I said. "What is it?"

"Last night, Alma Davis crashed his car in front of Grandma's farm!" she said. Alma Davis is well known in these parts as the meanest man in the county. He's been in and out of jail so many times that they say it equals his years on earth, and that's about forty. He's a short muscular man, dark complexion, with scars and tattoos all over his arms. His face is worn, with little black beady eyes, rotten teeth, a crooked nose from being broken so many times, and a big scar across his right cheek to top it all off. If anyone wants to know what a mean man is, just let 'em take a look at him. He lives up on Wolverton Mountain. They say he makes and sells 'shine for a livin'. It's rumored that he'll kill anyone who comes around. He'll even kill kids and feed 'em to his pack of killer hounds.

"Uncle Oscar went outside to help him get unstuck," Erma Lea said. "Alma was so belligerent

Chapter 6

that he started cursing Uncle Oscar! Then he raised his whiskey bottle to hit Uncle Oscar. Well, Uncle Oscar hit him in the mouth so hard he dropped the bottle and staggered all the way across the road and fell down into the ditch. I swear it's true," she said. "Grandma told Mama this morning."

I guess I must have been looking at her like she was making it all up. "Well," I said, "What happened next?"

She continued, "Uncle Oscar had knocked him out so he dragged him up to the porch by his shirt collar, covered him with a blanket, and left him on the porch all night."

"What happened when Alma woke up?" I asked.

"Well, this morning Uncle Oscar brought out some coffee to Alma; he drank it, went to his car and headed off up the mountain," she said. "He didn't speak or even look at Uncle Oscar."

"Well, that's something," I said, "but Uncle Oscar had better watch his back because now he's got two enemies on Wolverton Mountain, Lightfoot and Alma Davis!"

~~~~~

When December rolled around, every day was crisp and overcast, and the air was heavy. It snowed or drizzled freezing rain just about every day. Life

Holiday Hills

started becoming pretty slow. It would be this way for the next three months. Winter was always a slow time in the Ozarks. It seemed like forever as we waited for Christmas to arrive. Every day was long and dreary. We would bundle up like Eskimos and head down the trail to school, then spend eight dreary hours there and head back home again.

So when the twenty-fourth came, boy, were we excited! We sat around after supper and watched the fire crackle. Both Dana and I kind of shivered with excitement. Dad couldn't resist his usual joking and poking fun. He looked up from his book and said so seriously, "What are you two so excited about?"

"Dad, it's Christmas Eve," we responded.

"Oh," he said slyly. "I forgot about that." Then he started messing with us again. "I thought I heard sleigh bells, but Santa will probably go on by us because you kids are still up," he said, trying not to laugh.

We looked at each other, jumped up and ran to bed. It was the only time of the year where we weren't made to go to bed. Dad came and tucked us in. Dana and I stayed awake for awhile, talking softly and trying to see Santa out the window. A couple of times we thought we heard sleigh bells and sounds on the roof. But, we were too scared to

Chapter 6

look because we didn't want Santa to see us.

This year, I don't remember falling asleep. I woke up to Dad's whispers in my ear. "Santa came!" he said to both of us.

In a split second we were both up and running. When we entered the living room, we skidded to a stop. The tree was beautiful in the early morning light. Underneath were a dozen or more presents. Through the windows, we saw the hills covered with snow. All was white, and the Little Red was flowing down through the valley with snow falling into it. It sure was beautiful.

Dad ran in behind us saying, "Come look, girls! Santa ate some cookies and milk at the kitchen table. Come and look outside, and you'll see his footprints in the snow."

I'm not sure, and I didn't say anything, but it looked kinda like Dad's footprints. Dana believed him though, and Dad had a great twinkle in his eye.

"Let's start in on those presents!" he said laughing.

We started into them, separating them by name, shaking them and trying to guess what was inside.

Meanwhile, Dad sat back in his rocker with his housecoat on and pipe in his mouth. He loved it all. Somehow, I think he enjoyed it more than we did.

Holiday Hills

Mama woke up a little while later, dragged herself in, and sat down. She was not nearly as active and excited as Dad, but she never was. Mama fixed a good breakfast, and her best friend and next door neighbor, Sally Stovaugh, came over to sit and crochet with Mama. They had been trying to teach Dana and me to crochet. Little Sammy played on the floor with the wrapping paper - he just loved it. In his mind, every present was his. Every time one of us had a birthday, he thought it was his birthday. Counting the four of us, and some of our cousins, Little Sammy had about ten birthdays a year.

Dad cleaned up the kitchen for Mama. He was wearing her apron and washing dishes.

I laughed at him and said, "Dad you look funny."

"Don't you tell anyone about this or I'll be the laughingstock of Choctaw," he laughed. His face got kinda red, and I felt sorry for him. Dad was such a good man, always waiting on us kids and Mama. No other man ever treated his family as good as Dad treated us. We were truly blessed with him. He couldn't even whip us; Mama always whipped us when we needed it. Dad would try to talk to us about what we did wrong. He'd sit us on his lap and talk so sweet to us about our wrong doing - we

Chapter 6

couldn't stand it. He would kill us with kindness, so to speak. He'd always go out on the porch and cry when Mama whipped us.

Mama announced we would be going to Grandma's to spend Christmas night. This made us so happy - there's nothing like your Grandma's house. It was about six o'clock when we arrived and already dark because the sun set early in the winter.

Grandma had stockings filled with fruit and candy for us, hanging by the fireplace. Uncle Oscar brought wood in and built up the fire as we ate Christmas dinner. It was wonderful - turkey, potatoes, gravy, black eyed peas and cornbread. She had hot cherry and pumpkin pies on the stove. Man, it sure was good food. A couple of hours later, we were all quiet around the fire. It was so peaceful - it was magical.

Grandma started telling the story of Christ and the first Christmas, "Our Lord and Savior was born in a manger in Bethlehem, the City of David. Wise men came to worship Him and bring gifts. The three kings brought their most precious gifts from their countries. Shepherds were in the fields, guarding their flocks. A heavenly host came alive in the sky, singing praise to the Savior. 'Behold,' they said, 'In this night, a child is born; He is Christ, the Savior.

Holiday Hills

Peace on Earth and good will towards men!'" she finished.

As I sat there dreamy-eyed, I envisioned it all as if it had happened here in our hills. It was hard to imagine how far away Israel was and how long ago it all happened. Nineteen hundred, thirty-two years is a mighty long time for us, but Grandma said, 'One thousand years is like one day to our Lord.' Grandma always had a way of explaining things so that we kids could understand.

We slept on blankets in Grandma's living room by the fireplace. We drifted off to sleep to the crackle and pop of the fire. I awoke to the sound of Grandma and Mama fixin' breakfast and talking. There was coffee brewing on the stove, and Grandma offered me a cup.

"Sure," I said.

Mama said, "Mother, are you sure she's old enough to drink coffee?"

"Old enough, Grandma replied. "Why, I was married when I was her age, drinking coffee, chewing tobacco and plowing fields."

Grandma always seemed as old and wise as these hills. She and I have always had a special bond. It began the minute I was born. The doctor delivered me and was so tired he turned around

Chapter 6

and handed me to Grandma. Mama was so weak that she stayed in bed for weeks. Grandma did everything for me. I slept on her chest at night. She fed me with goat's milk. When Dad and Mama tried to take me home they said Grandma cried, but not as much as I did. I threw such a fit that they brought me back to stay another month. I love being with Dad and Mama, but there's no place like Grandma's.

The next day Dad went up to Clinton to get a mess of fireworks. He was so excited about the first of the year. He was a lot bigger kid than we were. We raked leaves all week long - piled and burned them. Dad was so antsy, he could hardly wait.

"How 'bout me popping a few?" he would ask Mama.

"No, Jim," she would say as if he were one of her kids asking to sample the dough before the cookies were made.

"Watch it," Dad yelled.

I ducked just as a bottle rocket zoomed past my head.

He looked at me seriously for a moment. When he saw I was all right, he fell to his knees in hysterical laughter.

I wasn't laughing - I was furious. I told him I

Holiday Hills

was going up to the house and sit in the swing. I never cared for fireworks anyway, and I had just as soon watch from up the hill. There were probably a dozen families down below our house on the Little Red, shooting fireworks. They were mighty pretty in the fading light.

After the fireworks were ended, I decided to put wood on the fire and help Mama fix a late night snack. Dad and Dana came up the hill a little after ten.

"Mom, that was fun," Dad said, "but it sure was cold! Made my throat and lungs hurt, breathing in that cold air. Better get into bed girls; school starts back tomorrow."

It was terribly cold outside the next morning. Arkansas doesn't usually have much cold weather. It was known mostly for its warm, humid climate. But when it did get cold, it cut you right down to the bone. And, this January was turning into a bone chiller! Most every day was in the forties while nights were in the teens and twenties. The wind blew every day, and we were having a lot of drizzle rain and sleet. I would take snow over that stuff any day!

Mama and Sally Stovaugh had made us both some gloves and boggins; they really kept out

Chapter 6

the cold. All of us kids loved it when it snowed and were thankful we had a white Christmas. But nobody liked a miserable January and February. Even Ole Lightfoot had disappeared from conversations. He wasn't raiding, and I don't know what he was eating to survive. Uncle Oscar said Lightfoot was up on Wolverton Mountain in his cave. He also told us that Lightfoot would make it through the winter because he was so tough.

One day after school, Dana, Erma Lea and I decided to go pond skating. It was so cold that most ponds had frozen solid. That didn't happen but every five or six years. We all got bundled up, tied the laces of the skates together and threw them over our shoulders. As we were about to leave, Mama yelled at Erma Lea, "Girl, where's your gloves and boggin?"

"I haven't got any, Aunt Clara," she said.

Mama nearly came unglued. "I'm gonna get your Mama and Daddy," she yelled. "Well, maybe you'll have some when you get in this evening," she said. When Mama told you something, it was the gospel.

When we got back at dark, Mama and Sally had made Erma Lea some gloves and a boggin just like she had promised. "I'll never let one of my kids do

Holiday Hills

without," Mama said.

Life went on, simple and boring during the next two months. But winter in Arkansas was always like that. People stayed in and rested. It was a chance to get ourselves ready for Spring when all the work started back. The routine of life here never changed much! Most of the excitement came from Lightfoot or Uncle Oscar. But, if January and February were boring in this part of the world, well March brought on hysteria!

Chapter Seven

Twister At Bee Branch

There was only one word in these parts that brought on fear and panic worse than the name of Lightfoot, and that was 'tornado'. Every year, March through May was like a war zone. Tornados always rolled into these hills from the Southwest. You never knew when they would pop up and form. The first tornado of the year hit over at Center Ridge, just up from Grandma's place. A family living on top of a mountain had just sit down to eat dinner. They noticed the hot sunny day had turned as black as night. They heard a noise like a freight

Twister at Bee Branch

train and saw the trees whipping savagely to and fro. Within a minute, before they could even move from the kitchen table, it was over. The house was completely gone. The father and one child survived; the mother and two other children did not. The tops of hills were bad places to live in this area because those twisters would bounce across the hilltops. Usually, the people in the valleys were safe from tornados. But if the county thought this was bad, it was nothing compared to what came in the last week of March. The entire community of Bee Branch was in for an awakening!

Bee Branch is located ten miles south of Choctaw on the road down to Conway and Little Rock. It was where Mama and Dad had lived for a couple of years before I was born. So naturally Mama and Dad had a lot of friends there. It was a real hot, humid day where the smoldering heat really gets to you. It was always like that before a storm. Everyone was sitting on their porches drinking cold water and lemonade and trying to catch a breeze. They could see the dark wall cloud headed up from the Southwest. The day became dead calm, and the sky turned to an eerie green color. I haven't witnessed this event up close. But, folks say that you'll swear the end of times are

Chapter 7

coming - the black clouds, the green sky and the super winds that level everything in their path. A few minutes before it hit, cows were bellowing in the fields. Horses were bucking and running, chickens were cackling and trying to fly off. A few of the old timers knew what was wrong and took shelter in some wine cellars. But the others got a quick lesson in the most devastating thing on earth. In another five minutes it was gone. Three people were found dead initially; three more were found later, and nearly a hundred were injured.

Dad and Uncle Oscar went down to help the community. When they got back, their stories were written on their faces. They both had looks as if they were sick at their stomachs - the way you look when you eat some sour apples. They told us that everything for a half mile wide was gone. Trees that were as big as fifty-five gallon drums were twisted off at the base. Cows were scattered all over, some still walking around in a daze. One cow was found grazing with a board stuck through it, as if it didn't realize it. A couple of people were sucked up into the eye of the tornado. They told of the most peaceful calm, and everything was green. Electricity bounced from side to side, and all kinds of debris swirled around. One lady was carried for a mile. She said, "I was flying through the air - looked around and a cow passed by, calm as it could be!" Dad said chickens were walking around unhurt, but had no feathers left on them. Forks and spoons were wedged into trees. One two by four was pushed through a tree and sticking out the other side. He said half the community was stripped of their clothing and had mud and dirt pressed upon their skin so tightly you couldn't tell they were naked. "It's difficult to understand the power of tornados; it's just terrible and I hope it's something I never have to witness again," he said. After that Dad never again talked about the Bee Branch tornado of 1933. But everyone else talked about it, that is, until Lightfoot started raiding again and gave them other things to talk about.

Chapter 8

Chapter Eight

Spring Time, Finally

Suddenly, everything just came to life. After nearly three months of some of the most boring time of my life, the world suddenly opened up and out came Spring. I was up out of my bed and looked across the countryside. The Little Red River Valley was alive with shades of orange, purple, pink, red and green. Every color in the rainbow was in those hills! I just couldn't believe it. It happens every year in April, but it always seems to come as a surprise for some reason - I think it's because winter is so bleak and gray. Not only was this the day that

Spring Time, Finally

Spring came alive, it was also my birthday, April 6th. Today, I would become a teenager - a whole, new life and a whole, new world.

Dad walked to the breakfast table, kissed me on the cheek and said, "Happy birthday, honey. What do you want to do today?"

Well that was an easy question to answer. "Go to Grandma's," I said quickly.

"Grandma's it is!" he exclaimed.

We ate and then headed over to Grandma's. She was on the porch when we pulled up. She got out of her rocker and hugged me, but didn't say anything about my birthday. That was funny because she had never forgotten it before. Come to think of it, Mama hadn't said anything to me either. No one had given me a present of any kind. My feelings were somewhat hurt, but I didn't expect anything. Maybe, they figured, since I was now thirteen I didn't need anything. Maybe that's the way it is when you get older. Mama and Dad didn't act like they were even going to come inside, but that was all right.

"Come on Dana," I yelled, "we'll go have some fun by ourselves." I couldn't believe the coldness of everyone. So I just went on into the house. As I walked in from the bright, warm sunlight, an explosion of song erupted. It made me jump!

Chapter 8

Everyone was there - all my family! There were over two dozen people consisting of cousins, aunts, and uncles - all had come to my birthday party. Erma Lea and her parents were also there. Even Uncle Oscar was standing in the back, trying to sing along. I was ashamed at myself for doubting them all.

Grandma brought out my cake and cookies. On the kitchen table was half a dozen presents. Tears swelled up in my eyes as Dad walked up behind me and put his arms around me. I was feeling gloomy at first, but this turned out to be the best birthday of my life. But little did I know that just hours away my view of life would drastically change. I was soon to find out the true evil side of this world. And likewise, I would find out the test of true love and commitment - the place where good and evil clash! I would find myself caught between the dark and the light.

We had our canteens full of water and our pouches full of cake and cookies. Erma Lea and Dana wanted to take an adventurous trip up on the southern side of Wolverton Mountain. I was initially leery of the idea, but finally gave in. As we started up the road to Wolverton Mountain, I made a compromise with Dana and Erma Lea. "We'll go

Spring Time, Finally

up on Wolverton, but let's go to the western side because Lightfoot's cave is on the eastern side," I said. They agreed. So we stayed on the road until we came to a small trail headed out to the west.

After being on the trail for about a quarter mile, we came up behind the most awful place I had ever seen in my life. There were bits and pieces of wagons and cars scattered all over the place. I couldn't see how anyone could get through that mess. A nasty shotgun shack was sitting right in the middle of this junk yard. The place reeked with odor. Old hound dogs lay all around the house. A small stream of smoke drifted up from the back of the house. There was a contraption that I recognized as a moonshine still. We could see a short, stocky man that I recognized as Alma Davis.

We hid behind a big rock, while I tried to figure out a good exit from this mess when Dana panicked, turned and tripped over an old steel bucket. It made a sound like thunder on the quiet mountain top. I gritted my teeth and motioned for them to stop and get down. When I looked up over the rock, I could see Alma already had a shotgun in his hands. Two half dressed, nasty looking women came out on the porch, and all the old hounds started coming to life. One old bloodhound, who must have been

Chapter 8

the leader, raised his nose up in the air and let out a long soulful howl. It must have been an alarm, because hounds came out of everywhere - from under the house, from under an old wagon, and out from the inside of old barrels. There were a dozen of them in all. Alma hollered for them to get after it. All the hounds started toward our direction. Alma fell in behind them.

"If somebody's out there, you're dead!" he screamed in a deep gravelly voice.

"Run!" I said in a shaky voice. "We must split up. Dana, you go left and Erma Lea, you go right; get back to Grandma's as fast as you can. Now go!"

They both took off as I went up the middle. I'll tell you what, those hounds might have been nasty looking, but they were pros about hunting - a dozen hounds split into three different directions. I couldn't believe what I was seeing. It was as if they did this sort of thing all the time. As soon as they started on our trails, the barking started. And, if you've ever heard a pack of hounds on a trail, it's a continuous noise that never seems to stop. It's not exactly a bark, and it's not exactly a howl; it's somewhere in between. Just knowing they're on your trail makes your blood run cold. I don't know why but Alma followed to the left, maybe sensing

Spring Time, Finally

Dana was an easier prey. I was heading down that mountain as fast as I could run and could hear Alma's hounds and his voice. He was cursing and swearing he would kill all of us. I knew why he was so mad; he didn't want anyone seeing him making moonshine. I couldn't stop and tell him we would promise not to tell anyone. I knew he would rather kill us than go back to jail. When I reached the base of the mountain, I stopped to catch my breath. I threw down my canteen and cookies. I needed to be as light as possible. I could hear hounds in all directions. My ears were ringing, and my heart felt like it was going to explode. I looked back and saw the hounds just a hundred feet away. I didn't see any sign of Erma Lea or Dana across the field. But, when I reached the back of Uncle Oscar's garden, I gave out. The hounds sure didn't; they were closing in fast. Hounds have a way of getting stronger as they go. I was trying to scream, but my mouth was so dry that I couldn't. I collapsed less than fifty yards from the house. I rolled over on my back. I could hear my heart beating so loudly that the barking of the hounds seemed a faint whisper. The blue sky seemed to be turning black. I was either passing out or the hounds had caught me, and I was dying. I could hear thunder, and the ground

Chapter 8

was shaking. I hadn't remembered any clouds forming in the sky. I closed my eyes and started to dream, in shock. I was dreaming about what had just happened; I didn't know if it was really real. I lost all consciousness and began to drift away - it was peaceful. All of a sudden, I was brought back to reality as a dozen hands were upon me, lifting me off the ground. I let out a scream and almost fainted again. Mama and Grandma put cold water over my neck and face. I looked around the crowd at everyone's shocked and pale faces. Erma Lea was there also. No one said a word.

"Erma Lea," I said. "Was that real?"

"Yes," she said. "I arrived just seconds before you did, and I gave the alarm!" "Where is Dana?" I asked.

Erma Lea's eyes swelled with tears. She just shook her head no.

I turned and looked toward Wolverton Mountain and there, in the edge of the garden, just some twenty feet away, were four dead hounds. I quickly turned toward the house and standing there was Uncle Oscar with his rifle held at his side. He had saved me. That was the thunder! It was not a dream! He turned and walked toward the barn.

After five minutes in the barn he emerged on top

Spring Time, Finally

of Ole Red. Rifle in hand, canteen across his saddle horn, they came over to us. Even Ole Red looked mad. He had the same piercing eyes that Uncle Oscar had when he got mad. He had a bounce in his walk. They came right up to our circle, Uncle Oscar not saying a word.

"Oscar," Grandma said. "Are you going to kill Alma Davis?"

"You damn right I am!" he said. He walked Ole Red briskly across the field toward Wolverton Mountain.

"There'll be blood in these hills tonight," Grandma said sadly.

Chapter 9

Chapter Nine

Blood On Wolverton Mountain

There was an eerie silence in Grandma's house. I had never felt anything like it before. Life is funny; this afternoon had been the happiest time of my life and now, I had a terrible knot in my throat, and my heart was heavy. No one said a word for over an hour. Mama and Grandma were trying to fix supper. The crickets and katydids were starting up as the light was fading. The evening was becoming incredibly dark; no moon seemed to be on the rise.

Erma Lea started talking about the hounds. "The hounds behind me backed off. I don't know why; I was pulling away from them pretty good, but I don't think that was the reason. There was a fight starting about the time I hit the garden. You likely didn't hear it, did you, Dena?" she asked.

"No," I said. "My ears were ringing, and my side was hurting so bad I couldn't have heard anything. You're made for running with those long legs," I said with a smile. "You didn't even seem tired."

She smiled and about that time it looked like Mama and Dad would break down and cry. That part about the fight must have really sounded bad to them. I wish Erma Lea hadn't said that, but I know she wasn't thinking. We ate supper in complete silence. Every few seconds one of use would look over at the clock; time passed so slowly. Every hour that passed seemed like a year; six hours seemed like six years.

Everyone was sitting in the living room about midnight when the front door burst open! Uncle Oscar stood there in the doorway like a giant. With his boots and hat he looked like he was seven feet tall! He stood motionless for a few seconds and then stepped forward with a grin across his face. Dana was asleep in his arms. He told her to wake up, and he bent over and put her down. "She's all right," he said.

Chapter 9

Everyone rushed to her. It appeared that she didn't have a scratch on her, yet she was traumatized.

Uncle Oscar hung up his hat and rifle and started across the kitchen toward his room.

"Oscar, is Alma Davis dead?" Grandma asked.

"Yes," he said as he turned and stood in the doorway to his room. "But, I didn't kill him." He gave a little smile, then turned and with a 'good night' to all, he closed his door.

The next morning, everyone looked mighty tired. We were all eating when Uncle Oscar emerged from his room, late for breakfast. All eyes were upon him when he sat down. He was clean shaven with his hair slicked back. He acted like he didn't even know why we were looking at him. We all knew he would kill Alma Davis, but he said he hadn't done it; that was just plain confusing. You could just feel the tension in the air.

He filled his plate and took a big sip of coffee before he started, "When I reached Alma's house, there wasn't no one there except a couple of nasty ole gals. I picked up Dana's trail and could hear a fight going on. It ended before I got there. When I arrived, I found Dana inside a big crack in the limestone. All around her were dead dogs, and

Alma was face down among them. I waded through the mess and grabbed Dana up. On the way back through it, I kicked Alma over, and his throat and guts were torn out. I knew what had happened, but I didn't ask Dana. Dana, would you like to tell us what happened?" he asked.

"Yes sir," she said. "The hounds were about to catch me, and Alma was right behind them. I knew I wasn't fast enough so I decided to climb up on a big rock. There was a huge rock surrounded by some smaller rocks and some big ole pine trees. I was jumping and clawing, trying to get up on that rock, and when I looked up, I saw a huge black cat stand up! I knew it had to be Lightfoot. He was aged looking with a lot of scars on him and had a bullet scar on his right shoulder. I knew that's where Uncle Oscar had shot him. He showed his fangs and just stared down at me with his yellow eyes. I turned and saw the hounds were up on the knoll; I had led them straight to Lightfoot. He squatted and jumped over my head, straight into them like a freight train. It seemed like almost an hour that they fought.

"I crawled into a crack in the limestone and watched them fight. The hounds had completely forgotten about me.

Chapter 9

"Halfway through the fighting, four more hounds joined in - eight dogs against Lightfoot, and he was winning. But it wasn't easy. He would have one dog down on his back, and then two or three other dogs would pile on him. He would then roll over and get those claws slashing like crazy. They fought back and forth, from one side of the knoll to the other. They fought up against the pines, and many times against the rock I was hiding in. At one time, their bodies covered up the crack in the rock. It scared me because I couldn't see anything.

"Alma was watching the whole thing, egging his dogs on. He kept trying to get a shot at Lightfoot, but knew with a shotgun he would also hit his dogs. Realizing his dogs were about finished, he laid the shotgun down and waded in with his Arkansas Toothpick; only two or three dogs remained in the fight. The others were scattered about, dead.

"Alma started in toward Lightfoot, screaming and cursing something awful. He was slashing that big knife from side to side. Lightfoot threw off the two dogs and tackled Alma Davis. They rolled twice, and Alma lay on his stomach, not moving.
"Lightfoot returned to one of the dogs and broke his neck. Another hound was barely alive and struggled to get up. Lightfoot pinned him down, clamping

down on his neck, suffocating him. He slowly rose up and walked around and through the crowd of dead bodies, seeming to check to make sure they were all dead. He had a lot of bad wounds and was very bloody. He was breathing very hard and had a terrible limp. He walked by the crack, stopped and looked in at me for a few seconds, trying to catch his breath. His eyes were trying to go shut; then he simply walked away. I let out a long sigh and closed my eyes. When I opened them, Uncle Oscar was standing there," she finished.

We all finished breakfast and got ready to go home. Grandma said a little prayer, thanking the Lord for watching over our family in this terrible situation.

Mama walked over, hugged Uncle Oscar and kissed him on the forehead as he drank his coffee. "Thank you brother," she said.

Uncle Oscar turned in his chair and said, "This time me and that cat are even. "I'll never bother him again. He's got my respect - he's a survivor!"

Chapter 10

Chapter Ten

The World Is Changing For Uncle Oscar

Uncle Oscar took the Sheriff up to where Alma was killed and gave his statement. Alma was buried in a lonely gravesite in the Halbrook Cemetery. An old copper headstone reading 'Rest In Peace' and his name were all that was on it. No one came to his funeral except Uncle Oscar, the Sheriff and Preacher - I guess no one cared that he was gone. He had lived a mean life and died a mean, violent death. The Good Book tells us that if you live by the sword, you will die by the sword. I guess

The World Is Changing for Uncle Oscar

that has to be true.

Soon, everything calmed down. It was May when Uncle Oscar announced he would go up on the mountain for a day or two.

"What for?" Grandma asked.

"I've got my own reasons," he said. Uncle Oscar never told you what was on his mind, at least not 'til he had checked things out first. So we didn't think it was funny when he rode out on Ole Red one afternoon.

Dana and I had spent the night with Grandma while Uncle Oscar was gone. We were making homemade ice cream the next day when Uncle Oscar rode up on Ole Red. He came over to the porch, sat down and rocked back and forth while staring out at the road.

"Well tell us what's on your mind boy, or you'll kill me with curiosity!" Grandma exclaimed.

He turned and looked at us for a second, then looked back at the road. He never looked at a person very much, but he never missed anything either. Then he proceeded to tell us his story while he stared at the road, "I knew the fight was very hard on Lightfoot. And you know, we haven't heard anything from him in a month. So I just went up to his cave and found him dead, just like I figured I

Chapter 10

would. He made it through that fight, won, and then made it back to his home and died honorably! Yes, he sure did!"

I swear that he looked like he had tears in his eyes.

"Let's keep this between us," he said. "I don't want people going up there snooping around. Let Lightfoot lay in peace. He's a great legend around here, and folks probably wouldn't accept his death anyhow - legends are not supposed to die. Man, I've lost both of my enemies within a month of each other. I don't know what I'll do with all this time on my hands," he said sarcastically.

He got up and walked slowly toward the barn. I don't know why, but he seemed very sad. Maybe he felt like he was becoming the last of the old rough bunch. This world was becoming more civilized all the time, and Uncle Oscar was not a part of the new world. He was a figure of the past when everyone rode on horses and mules; when men settled their problems with a Winchester and an Arkansas Toothpick; when bears and wolves ruled the nights; when you survived off the land. There were no game laws and no lawmen waiting to get you for every little thing you did. Uncle Oscar never learned to write and could barely read. But,

The World Is Changing for Uncle Oscar

in this new world he had to learn; he had to become civilized. I guess Alma Davis and Lightfoot were the last remaining ties he had to the old ways. To us, it was terrible, but to Uncle Oscar it must have been comforting. Now, he seemed to feel all alone. This was a man who was fifty years old and had never been married. He had always lived at the farm, hunting and fishing. When he was young he had worked for a short while as a deputy in Fort Smith. Everyone knew those men were tough because they had to go into the Oklahoma Badlands and round up the worst of criminals. Rapists and murderers, they all went to Oklahoma to hide out. We couldn't help him with his sadness.

Grandma told us to leave him alone. "A tough man like him has to take care of his pain alone." I guess that's so.

Chapter Eleven

*A Year In The Life
Of An Ozark Girl*

We went back home and got ready for the last day of school and the graduation ceremony. Erma Lea was president of our class and I was secretary, so we both had to give speeches. When it was my turn, I was on shaky legs. There were a few hundred people there. My speech was one I had written about God, country and how proud I was to be an American living in Arkansas. I looked out and spotted all my family. Mama was holding Little Sammy, and he was waving at me. Dad had a huge grin on his face, and Grandma was in a new dress that she had made for this occasion. Erma Lea's family was there also. I jumbled my words and started looking around, very embarrassed. The door in the back of the auditorium opened, and a huge figure stood there dressed in black boots, black hat, blue jeans and a flannel shirt - it was Uncle Oscar! He came in, looked around awkwardly and took off his hat while smiling at me. My heart was so big inside, I thought it would burst through my chest. Uncle Oscar may not have been a part of the new world, but he was trying to embrace it.

I finished my speech, and everyone applauded. So ended my seventh grade year of school. I looked out at the crowd and realized what a wonderful family God had blessed me with. I looked at them with such love, and tears filled my eyes. And I knew there was no other place I would rather be than here, in Formosa.